Laughing
YOUR
LIFE
Healthy

Brenda M. Hardwick

Denver, CO.

brendahardwickauthor@gmail.com

Active Member, RMFW, CAL

Laughing Your Life Healthy

Copyright © 2017 by *Brenda M. Hardwick*

ISBN
978-1-957895-37-6 (Paperback)
978-1-957895-36-9 (eBook)

Dedication

This book is dedicated to my sons Ivan & James Jackson, thank you for believing in your Mom, all of my grandchildren-Shante', Kris, & Jordyn, your childhood laughter will always live in my memory, and the ones on the way-I can't wait to hear you laugh!!

ACKNOWLEDGMENTS

Thanks to The Creator and Divine Source for blessing me with the gift of these words to share. Thank you to all of my friends who listened to me talk about this book for the last year. Thank you to those who read and edited: Markie Davis, my son Dr. James P. Jackson, my Son-in-love Brian Goodrow Jackson, Suzanne Kubec, Jess Mason and Esther Meehan, your suggestions, critiques and edits were invaluable! I also thank The Institute of Integrative Nutrition for helping me grasp the synchronicity that flows through my life. Lookout! Here come the Ripples!

> *"IF WE COULDN'T COULDN'T LAUGH WE WOULD ALL GO INSANE."*
>
> — **Robert Frost**

INTRODUCTION

As I grew older, I got more serious about life, about living, about... everything. I've survived two brushes with diseases or ailments that could have taken me out. See what being *serious* gets you? But, I'm still here, and I realized that things were better when I laughed more. And it had been a very long time since I had really laughed, and paid attention to laughing.

In 2010 I weighed 210 lbs., had very high cholesterol (over 400!), Irritable Bowel Syndrome, Over-active Bladder, Sarcoidosis, and self-diagnosed celiac disease. My feet, knees, and body hurt all over, and having been a caretaker for three different people, reality slapped me. I was headed towards being really sick again. I didn't feel good, didn't look good (at least to me) and heard my change towards the negative being reflected in the comments of others; "Where's the Brenda I used to know?"

After attending an insurance conference, where I participated in a session of Laughter Yoga, along with other health related wakeup calls, synchronicity began to occur with some regularity and I started my journey towards my healthy destination. Incorporating more laughter into my life, and the lives of others, became the foundation for making change in my life, and I decided to make laughter part of my giving back to humanity. As a Certified Integrative Nutrition Health Coach, Laughter Yoga Leader, and Seraphic Energy Practitioner, I am causing ripples that will guide people to find their light, lift their life, and shine their health!

If everyone who reads this book laughs a little more, and a little longer than before, I've completed my mission!

CONTENTS

"LAUGHTER IS
GOOD FOR YOU.
NINE OUT OF
TEN STAND-UP
COMEDIANS
RECOMMEND
LAUGHTER
IN THE FACE
OF INTENSE
STUPIDITY."

— Jim Butcher,
Proven Guilty

WHAT'S THE PROBLEM?

The problem is… (hands on the table drumroll) We don't laugh. That's it, that's the problem, in three words, or a nutshell. We don't laugh. And laughter is just one of the many important elements of a healthy life. You're thinking… Laughter… really? Laughing is important? Yes, laughter *is* important!

Maybe it's a little unfair to say that we don't laugh. Some folks do laugh, and as often as possible, however, they are in the minority.

In response to hearing the statement "We Don't Laugh", some people will say "But I laugh all the time!" And, they *think* they do! People think they laugh, and that they are laughing a lot. But if you actually count how many times in a day you laugh, you will most likely be very surprised at how low that number is. So let's test my theory.

> ## "LAUGHTER IS AN INSTANT VACATION."
>
> — Milton Berle

HOW MANY TIMES A DAY DO YOU LAUGH?

This is the first question for you to answer: How many times a day do *you* Laugh? Keep a tally. For one day, every time you laugh, make a mark on a sheet of paper. Use sticky notes. They are everywhere and you can use them throughout the day and then count them all up before bed. See how many laughs actually come out of you.

The answer to this question will vary from person to person. People, who are already aware and are paying attention, will laugh more. Many people will fail to rise to this challenge because they think they don't need to know, or that it doesn't matter. But, everyone needs to have an idea of how much they really laugh, so they know how much more they need to incorporate into their day.

In reality, if you consciously keep track, most adults only laugh an average of 15 times a day. Now, there's no pressure here, and no guilt being flung to the masses. This is an observation of what is found to be most common.

In comparison, toddlers laugh about 300-500 times a day… Three hundred times a day! Whoa! What happened to us? When did we lose our ability to laugh… at ourselves? At life's comedy? With each other? And, laughter is contagious!! Or, at least it used to be.

There are many reported incidents of punishment being meted out as a result of laughing out loud. I can remember being *written up* myself during a performance review, for laughing too loudly on one of my jobs. I always wondered who complained; I would have liked the opportunity to follow-up with them!

I've heard people complain about others saying, "She laughs all the time!" or "She laughs about everything!"or "Everything is funny to him/her!" with anguish, distaste, or even disgust. When did laughing become such a bad thing?

Think about it. How many times have you been told to *shush* when laughing? When did laughing become so inappropriate?

While this sounds and seems like a ridiculous occurrence, it is something that happens every day, and far too often. After all, who doesn't like to laugh? Then again, if you give it some thought, we have been programmed from a very young age, *not* to laugh, and especially out loud.

It is about at the age of two that adults innocently begin to shush little ones when they laugh. It's usually not as insidious as it sounds, and sometimes with seemingly good reason and intention that it happens.

Children laugh with spontaneity, and at everything, and everywhere they are. Even as babies we laugh! Sometimes adults see laughter as inappropriate... and who told us that? For example: in church, in libraries, in school, at the dinner table – uh, you can't laugh at dinner? Eating must be a serious activity! There's also when adults are engaged in what they consider a *serious* discussion. I bet you can think of many other examples.

When my grandsons were little, about ages 2 and 4, there was an animated commercial with a little yellow car that beeped, followed by the slogan, "TV Taxi..." They would hear it and laugh until they couldn't breathe! When I asked what was so funny, they would look at each other, and start laughing again! I never got an answer. It was sheer, unadulterated joy for joy's sake. And they could do it for no reason... I miss that! I miss hearing their laughter, and I miss being able to *do* that! Sadly, now that they are both young adults, when I asked what was so funny back then, they don't remember, and their *spontaneous* laughter is now usually no more than an embarrassed giggle. I really hope that I can help them, and you, recapture some of that childhood spontaneity and be able laugh with abandon again.

> ## "A DAY WITHOUT LAUGHTER IS A DAY WASTED."
>
> — Charlie Chaplin

WHEN IS THE LAST TIME YOU LAUGHED TODAY?

Laughter is amazing! It can make a difference in how you approach everyday issues, even the ones that trigger negative emotions. So, question two is: When is the last time you laughed today? I mean *really* laughed? *Today!* Did you laugh this morning, when you woke up? How about at lunchtime? Did you laugh on the way home from work? Maybe after you got home from work? Was there any laughter during dinner? Did you hear anybody else laughing today and wonder what was so funny? Did it make you smile?

I don't know about you, but some days I have to make an extra effort to laugh. Stuff just isn't funny on some days. It is very encouraging to know that your brain doesn't distinguish between *real* laughter, and just going through the motions.

You're thinking, "So, I can just say ha, ha, ha, and it still works?" Yes! Exactly! What this means is that when stuff isn't funny, you don't have to search for something funny to *make* yourself laugh. Not that there is anything wrong with searching laughter out. In fact, there are many sources available on the Internet, like You Tube, where you can find funny stuff to make you laugh. But, what if you just don't *feel* like laughing? What then?

What is really amazing about your brain and laughter is that because your brain can't tell the difference between *real* laughter and pretend laughter, it still produces all of the positive results. A by-product of *pretending* to laugh is that real laughter is typically triggered because a little laughter makes for more laughter. Even your own laughter is contagious!

> *"THE MOST WASTED OF ALL DAYS IS ONE WITHOUT LAUGHTER."*
>
> — E.E. Cummings

WHEN IS THE LAST TIME YOU LAUGHED SO HARD YOUR STOMACH HURT?

Laughing until your stomach hurts… what is typically called a belly laugh. Have you had one recently? Question three is: When is the last time you laughed so hard your stomach hurt? Or maybe you laughed until you started coughing? Or you laughed until you cried? All of these are valid measures of a good, cleansing laugh. The kind of laugh you tell others about, and laugh again in the retelling.

Laughing this hard may need a catalyst, like watching a funny a movie, or listening to your favorite comedian, but it's still a good thing. My favorite laughter moment; well there are two. One is from a movie and one is from a TV show. First, the Movie "The Money Pit" starring Tom Hanks and Shelley Long; the scene where the turkey explodes from the oven, or when the bathtub falls through the floor - hilarious!!!! Always makes me laugh to tears! And the other is an episode from The Carol Burnett Show - the one where Tim Conway tells the story about the Siamese elephants, joined at the trunk. I laugh again just thinking about that one! If you've never seen these gems, rent the movie, and you can Google the Carol Burnett episode on the Internet.

I have found that finding the funny in every day occurrences may take a little practice. Especially if you are a person that feels that you just don't, or can't laugh.

A person who doesn't laugh, or smile, for that matter… do people like this actually exist? Yes, they do. I've heard people say "I don't smile" or "I don't laugh" and they really believe that they are incapable of smiling and laughing. First of all, whatever you believe, *Is,* no matter what it is. So a person, who believes that they don't smile or laugh, doesn't. It is a self-fulfilling prophecy. I personally feel it is a tragedy that anyone feels this way. Everyone should be able to give themselves the positive feelings and health benefits of laughing.

"I DON'T TRUST ANYONE WHO DOESN'T LAUGH."

— Maya Angelou

FOOD FOR THOUGHT

Laughter has a long list of health benefits. Here is the short list, just to name a few:

Physical - Laughter boosts your immune system and relaxes your muscles.

Mental – Laughter raises your emotional intelligence and reduces anxiety, fear and stress.

Social – Laughter strengthens relationships and defuses conflict.

There are so many reasons to laugh, and this is by no means an all-inclusive list!

Laughter is part of being an animal. Studies show that humans are not the only animals that laugh – chimpanzees, gorillas, orangutans, and rats are some of the other animals that we *know* laugh. This means that all of us *can* laugh and smile, but for reasons unknown, some people choose not to. I would speculate that people who believe that they don't or can't laugh or smile have had some trauma connected with laughter, most likely something from their childhood.

Eeeeerrrrrrk! Let's put the brakes on! It's getting awfully deep here…

At this point, I encourage you to keep reading, especially if you are one of those folks who feel that you don't, or can't laugh or smile. These words won't cure you, however, if you want to learn a way to start laughing, without therapy, stay tuned; your first recipe for laughing is coming up!

If you have realized that you haven't been laughing as much as you used to, I encourage you to keep reading too. Learning that you've lost your joy, especially when you didn't know it was gone, can be a shocking realization, and the upcoming laughter recipes will jumpstart your healing process and help you find your joy again.

"YOU CAN'T
DENY
LAUGHTER;
WHEN IT COMES,
IT PLOPS
DOWN IN YOUR
FAVORITE CHAIR
AND STAYS AS
LONG AS IT
WANTS."

— Steven King

WHY LAUGHTER IS SO IMPORTANT — OK, HERE'S THE SCIENCE...

Laughing is an essential part of a healthy life. Laughing uses your whole body. A good, sustained laugh uses almost every part of your brain; the frontal lobe, limbic system, cerebral cortex-left and right, hippocampus and the occipital lobe, another words, at least some part of every section of your brain participates.

There are the other body parts: lungs, heart, stomach, diaphragm, and almost every muscle, that also reap the benefits provided by laughing. Starting at the top, with the face, laughing can give the body a workout. In fact, one minute of sustained laughter is equal to ten minutes on a rowing machine... I think I'd rather laugh for a minute than use a rowing machine for ten!

Laughter is good for you inside and out! You're thinking, "What do you mean *inside?*"

Laughter raises your endorphin and serotonin levels in your body. Ok, so I know you're thinking, what does *that* mean? It means that laughter causes a real, positive chemical reaction in your brain and body.

Serotonin is important for regulation of mood, appetite and sleep. Serotonin also has some cognitive functions, including memory and learning. Serotonin is found in your gut..., which, incidentally, is where the majority of your immune system lives, and your central nervous system, including your brain, which controls everything.

Endorphins, on the other hand, have long been associated with exercise and the rush of feeling good that exercise produces in a person. That rush is from the body's production of endorphins, another chemical produced by the brain and central nervous system. Endorphins are connected with feeling good... I mean really good! The effects of natural endorphin release is your target with increasing your laughter. This is a better alternative to the unhealthy, abnormal proportions of endorphin release that some drugs will produce in a person. The difference is that you produce the endorphins through the natural, biological processes of your body, and you can make it happen without leaving your home, endangering your life, or spending any money.

In the last few years, scientists have studied laughter and it has been proven that laughter produces endorphins. Another plus, endorphins are also known to block pain.

Wait.... What? Endorphins block pain? Yes, yes they do! And, laughing raises endorphin levels. So, laugh... out loud, and as often as you can, especially if something hurts, or if you're feeling down.

"ALWAYS LAUGH WHEN YOU CAN, IT IS CHEAP MEDICINE."

— George Gordon Byron

HOW TO INCORPORATE MORE LAUGHTER INTO EVERYDAY

There are many avenues to incorporating more laughter into your day. There are really no specific rules to this, and you are free to choose what method works for you. It may not be the same thing that works for your friends, or your family, and that's okay! Everyone has had different challenges and experiences that have slowly eroded both the importance of, and the occurrence of laughter in their lives.

Many years ago I was having difficulties with the "office politics" at my job. Without realizing it happened, I had lost my joy. When I started my career, I was the one who kept my co-workers laughing when the work we were doing was anything but fun and happy work. Shortly after changing employers, I was diagnosed with cancer. I survived, physically, but what I didn't see coming was the toll it took on my spirit. Over the next several years I slowly became just another one of the unhappy, frowning, often reduced to tears by the comments of others, people who I had always tried to bring a smile to. And, I wasn't laughing anymore. It was a crisis of personal values that made me see how much I had changed. Looking around me, at the people in my life, I realized I wasn't the only one suffering from a lack of joy. I made it my mission to change that, beginning with myself.

"LAUGHTER IS POISON TO FEAR."

— George R.R. Martin,
A Game of Thrones

THE AVAILABLE TOOLS

There are several methods that are being used today to increase the amount of laughter people experience. The role that laughter serves in healing is being documented much more often in today's science and literature.

The first method I will discuss is Laughter Yoga. Virtually everyone who hears the term for the first time hasn't a clue as to what Laughter Yoga is. Most people jump to a conclusion and want to equate it with some type of *standard* Yoga practice, like vinyasa, or hot yoga. The brainchild of Dr. Madan Kataria, a physician from Mumbai, India, Laughter Yoga is a discipline where people gather, typically in a park or other open space, or suitable sized room, and a Laughter Leader guides the group through laughter exercises. Unlike a traditional yoga practice, Laughter Yoga is laughter, pure and simple. This practice is a way to learn how to add laughter into your life, when laughter is missing. There is no need to be on the floor, no yoga pants or yoga mat needed. It is laughter, with a purpose. This is a great way to join others in a group setting on a guided laughter journey.

Another method available for guided group laughter is Laughter Therapy, which "aims to use the natural physiological process of laughter to help relieve physical or emotional stresses or discomfort." Laughter Therapy is now being used in the treatment of mental health issues, cancer, stress reduction, and the list continues to grow.

Individual methods of increasing laughter in your life include Comedy. Whether it is listening to your favorite comedian, or watching funny movies or television programs, you can find what makes you laugh and use it to raise your laughter quotient.

Modern technology allows for recording your favorite comedy for immediate playback, whenever you want or need it!

It has been documented by many how laughter helps cure disease. My research indicates that science still doesn't give laughter the credit it should, but the list of people who believe that laughter helps cure, is growing on a daily basis.

"IT IS CHEERFUL
TO GOD WHEN
YOU REJOICE
OR LAUGH
FROM THE
BOTTOM OF
YOUR HEART."

— Martin Luther King Jr.

PROMISES KEPT

Earlier I promised you that I would give you some ways to begin your laughter journey. Yes, journey. That's what this will be. It happens at the point in our lives where we realize that we need to do something, to change things. When we realize that we let somebody steal our joy, and we need to get it back. Increasing our laughter is one easy way to start. Using comedy is highly recommended, and it is readily available and accessible to nearly everybody in one form or another. Whether it's a live show, a trip to the theater, or movies, renting a movie, watching TV, or the Internet, comedy is all around us.

Suggested movies and television to make you laugh: (Please note; these are only my suggestions, and some of them are not rated PG. So please Google them first. We're after laughter, not shock and awe!) Disclaimer: I realize that some of these suggestions may be a bit dated; Boomers will recognize many of the titles, X'ers, and Millennial's may not be familiar with them, however, the Internet provides the resources to find them if you want to check them out. And, of course, anything current that makes you laugh hard enough to bring tears, you can add to the list!

Movies:

The Money Pit

Bridesmaids

Spaceballs

Groundhog Day

History of the World, Part I

Despicable Me (all of them!)

Blazing Saddles

Airplane

Duck Soup (Marx Brothers)

Monty Python and The Holy Grail

Coming To America

The Jerk

Caddyshack

Stir Crazy

Abbot & Costello Meet Frankenstein

The Nutty Professor (and anything else with Jerry Lewis in it!)

The Producers

Police Academy

Best In Show

Friday

Television:

The Carol Burnett Show

MASH

The Wayans Brothers

The Jeffersons

All In The Family

Roseanne

The Mary Tyler Moore Show

Everybody Hates Chris

Police Squad

Reno 911

Married With Children

Friends

Scrubs

Night Court

Modern Family

Newhart

Will & Grace

Sanford & Son

The Golden Girls

The Bernie Mac Show

The Honeymooners

I Love Lucy

The Abbott & Costello Show

The Three Stooges

The Larry Saunders Show

Cheers

The Fresh Prince Of Bellaire

Parks & Recreation

Taxi

The Office

Martin

Seinfeld

30 Rock

Arrested Development

WKRP in Cincinnati

The Tonight Show with Jimmy Fallon (or whoever is hosting!)

Late Night with Seth Meyers (or whoever is hosting!)

This method of provoking your own laughter does rely heavily on you having a sense of humor, and finding the images, jokes, and physical comedy funny. However a sense of humor and finding things funny is not necessary to get the desired result, which is to laugh.

Remember how I said earlier that the brain doesn't know the difference between real laughter and fake laughter? The following are three "Laughter Recipes" to get your laugh on, even if you don't feel like laughing.

When using these *recipes*, it is recommended that you have a mirror and look at your eyes in your reflection. While looking in your eyes, send yourself Love, and any other positive thoughts you can think of!

Warning: **Nothing negative allowed!!!** When those negative thoughts try to sneak in, think *Love*. The word alone can have a calming effect on how and what you are thinking.

"YOU DON'T STOP LAUGHING BECAUSE YOU GROW OLD. YOU GROW OLD BECAUSE YOU STOP LAUGHING."

— Michael Pritchard

RECIPES

Recipe One – Just Going Through The Motions

Ingredients:

Clapping (open handed, fingertips touching)

2 Ha's Ho's, & Hee's (as directed)

Deep Breaths (in through your nose, out through pursed lips)

1 Mirror (Optional)

Timer (Optional)

Instructions:

While looking at your reflection in the mirror (If you have one)-concentrate on your eyes repeat the following sequence for at least one minute (approximately 25 times):

While clapping say: "Ho ho, ha ha, hee hee, 1; ho ho, ha ha, hee, hee, 2" etc. to 25

Breathe in to the count of 5, then out through pursed lips to the count of 5 –

10 times

Repeat twice, at least two times per day.

Total time = approximately 1 minute 15 seconds per session

> "I KNOW WHY
> WE LAUGH.
> WE LAUGH
> BECAUSE IT
> HURTS, AND IT'S
> THE ONLY THING
> TO MAKE IT
> STOP HURTING."
>
> — Robert A. Heinlein

RECIPE TWO – HA MEANS PEACE

The word Ha is part of the words for Peace in the languages of Mala in West Africa, Kurdish, Tahitian, and Aymara in Bolivia. In Hawaiian, Ha means Breath of Life.

Ha can be said in any tone of voice and still have a positive effect on your mood.

Ingredients:

Lots of Ha's

Clapping to match

Timer and/or Mirror (optional)

Instructions:

While looking at your reflection (concentrate on your eyes), begin clapping in time with saying the Ha's -

1 Single Ha's (Ha) 10 times

2 Double Ha's (Ha ha) 10 times

3 Triple Ha's (Ha ha ha) 10 times

4 Quadruple Ha's (Ha ha ha ha) 10 times

3 Triple Ha's (Ha ha ha) 10 times

2 Double Ha's (Ha ha) 10 times

1 Single Ha's (Ha) 10 times

Breathe - in to the count of 5, then out through pursed lips to the count of 5 - 5 times

Do this once in the morning, once at lunchtime, once at dinnertime, once before bed.

Total time = approximately 1 minute per session

"IT IS
IMPOSSIBLE
FOR YOU TO
BE ANGRY
AND LAUGH
AT THE SAME
TIME. ANGER
AND LAUGHTER
ARE MUTUALLY
EXCLUSIVE
AND YOU HAVE
THE POWER
TO CHOOSE
EITHER."

— Wayne Dwyer

RECIPE 3 — I DON'T WANT TO LAUGH TODAY

Ingredients:

Mirror

Clapping

Ha's

Tune of your choice (optional)

Instructions:

While looking in the mirror (concentrate on your eyes) and clapping, to the tune of your choice, say the following:

I don't want to laugh today — ha ha ha ha ha — repeat 2 more times

Breathe - in to the count of 5, then out pursed lips to the count of 5 - 2 timesWhile looking in the mirror (concentrate on your eyes) and clapping, say:

You can't make me laugh today — ha ha ha ha ha — repeat 2 more times

Breathe - in to the count of 5, then out pursed lips to the count of 5 - 2 times

While looking in the mirror (concentrate on your eyes) and clapping, say:

Guess I will laugh anyway – ha ha ha ha ha – repeat 2 more times

Breathe - in to the count of 5, then out pursed lips to the count of 5 - 2 times

Total time = approximately 1 minute per session

"CARRY LAUGHTER WITH YOU WHEREVER YOU GO."

— Hugh Sidey

CONCLUSION

These recipes will get you started laughing. They are easy to do and most everyone will have all of the *ingredients* on hand. I've given the counts as well as the times, so… you *can* do this!

Try it for a week. You can use only one of the recipes or a combination of all three. Make a note of how you are feeling about your life before you start, and then again at the end of the week. The difference you feel will encourage you to keep going!

You really can Laugh Your Life Healthy!

"AT THE HEIGHT
OF LAUGHTER,
THE UNIVERSE
IS FLUNG INTO A
KALEIDOSCOPE
OF NEW
POSSIBILITIES."

— Jean Houston

REFERENCES

Humor and Stress: Laugh Your Way to Better Health

www.medicalcenter.virginia.edu/feap/work-life/.../Humor%20 and%20Stress.pdf

Scientists Hint At Why Laughter Feels So Good
NY Times James Gorman Sept. 13, 2011

THE BLOG
Hacking Into Your Happy Chemicals: Dopamine, Serotonin, Endorphins and Oxytocin

10/20/2014 11:56 am ET | Updated Dec 20, 2014 Huffington Post

Laughter
From Wikipedia, the free encyclopedia

How Laughter Works
BY MARSHALL BRAINSCIENCE | EMOTIONS

Laughter is the Best Medicine
The Health Benefits of Humor and Laughter

ABOUT THE AUTHOR

After spending 30 years in the world of Workers' Compensation, Brenda Hardwick wanted to really help people in a way that workers' comp can't. Bringing Laughter back into the lives of others is one of the ways to meet her mission objective. Brenda is the Owner of The Light Of Nature, LLC, a CIN Health Coach, Laughter Yoga Leader, and Seraphic Energy Practitioner. She believes that Everyone has a Light to Shine!

www.TheLightOfNature.com

Your Light, Your Life, Your Health, Better!